T0395023

AVALANCHES

Dalton Rains

Library of Congress Control Number: 2025930297

ISBN
979-8-89250-658-8 (hardcover)
979-8-89250-693-9 (ebook pdf)
979-8-89250-676-2 (hosted ebook)

Printed in the United States of America
Mankato, MN
082025

NOTE TO PARENTS AND EDUCATORS

Apex books are designed to build literacy skills in striving readers. Exciting, high-interest content attracts and holds readers' attention. The text is carefully leveled to allow students to achieve success quickly.

TABLE OF CONTENTS

Chapter 1

WINTER WARNING

A major winter storm approaches a mountain. Strong winds whip through the trees. Suddenly, there's a loud cracking sound. A large tree falls to the ground. The tree pushes snow down the mountain. It's an avalanche!

Avalanches can strike with very little warning.

The avalanche picks up more and more snow. It slides toward a road far below. Nearby devices sense movement and sounds. They detect the avalanche. They send out warnings. Flashing lights warn drivers. Electronic signs show messages.

DRIVING DANGERS

Highway closures help keep cars off the road during avalanches. Sometimes, highways may close hours or days before an avalanche happens. Other times, short-notice warnings stop nearby drivers.

During an avalanche, signs may warn drivers that roads are closed.

ROAD CLOSED
AVALANCHE CONTROL

Seconds later, the avalanche tumbles across the highway. It covers the road with heavy snow. Rocks and fallen trees crash down, too. The debris piles more than 4 feet (1.2 m) high. But the road is clear of cars. The warnings have kept people safe.

CLEANUP CREWS

After an avalanche, crews work quickly. They use plows to clear snow from the road. They also remove unstable snow from the mountainside.

Roads remain closed to traffic until they are plowed.

A large avalanche can destroy everything in its path.

Chapter 2

ALL ABOUT AVALANCHES

Avalanches happen when large amounts of snow, ice, and rocks fall down a mountain. Avalanches only form under certain conditions. They need snow, a steep slope, and a trigger.

Avalanches are most common in the first 24 hours after a heavy snowfall. The slides can be triggered in several ways. Some avalanches start after a sudden change in weather. Others are caused by the collapse of an icy overhang. People on skis or snowmobiles may also trigger avalanches.

STRONG SOUNDS

In rare cases, sound can cause an avalanche. Strong sound waves can shift snow. The human voice is not loud enough. But loud airplanes may start a slide.

The weight and vibration of a snowmobile can trigger an avalanche.

Avalanches come in different sizes. Some are small. Light, powdery snow gets released. Other times, avalanches are large. Huge sections of packed snow break free. A large avalanche can have one million tons of snow.

An avalanche may travel more than 150 miles per hour (240 km/h).

SLAB AVALANCHES

Over time, new snowfalls create different layers on a mountainside. Some layers have loose snow. Other layers have snow that is stuck together, or bonded. A bonded layer may slide over a loose layer. That is called a slab avalanche.

Avalanches often block or damage roads. They can cover railways, too. Some even push over trains. Avalanches can also damage buildings. They may kill people.

1916 AVALANCHE

History's deadliest avalanche happened in 1916. It took place in Italy. During World War I (1914–1918), many soldiers fought there. A huge avalanche buried a camp in the mountains. At least 270 people died.

Avalanches can easily destroy vehicles.

Rescue workers try to save people who are buried in avalanches.

Danger does not end when an avalanche stops moving. The snow compacts. It hardens like concrete. People who are stuck inside cannot dig out. The thick snow makes breathing difficult or impossible.

SNOW SPORTS

Skiers and snowboarders can be caught in avalanches. They may get stuck. About 200 skiers die in avalanches every year.

WINTER OF TERROR

Europe's worst avalanche season happened in late 1950 and early 1951. That season was called the "Winter of Terror." For months, heavy snow fell in the Alps. Strong winds blew through the mountains, too. The winds caused huge snow drifts. The snow became unstable. Avalanches happened all through winter.

The avalanches buried entire villages. Hundreds of people died. Many homes were damaged. A train station was destroyed, too.

The "Winter of Terror" affected Italy, Austria, and Switzerland.

Chapter 3

BASIC TESTS

At first, people tried to predict avalanches using basic observations. They looked for warning signs. For instance, they looked for the cracks that form on the surface of unstable snow. They also listened. Walking over unstable snow may create hollow thumping sounds.

After snow cracks, it may glide down the mountain.

Checking the snow's layers takes only a few minutes.

People also used simple tests. They could tap on a section of snow with a shovel. Sometimes, the snow collapsed easily. That showed an avalanche was possible. Other times, people dug pits in the snow. That way, they could study the snow's layers. Some layers were made of ice crystals. These meant an avalanche was more likely.

SIMPLE TOOLS

Simple tools helped people find dangerous areas. Avalanches are most likely to happen when the mountainside is at a certain angle. So, people used inclinometers. These tools measure the slope's angle.

People also built structures for protection. For instance, they built new retaining walls. Some were placed near buildings and roads. Others were on mountain slopes. Higher up, people built fences. They also placed snow nets. These nets stopped dangerous layers of snow from forming.

Fences can make the snow move in specific directions.

TREE WALLS

Trees act as natural retaining walls. Areas with no trees tend to have more avalanches. So, logging can create dangerous areas. To help prevent avalanches, people can plant new trees.

In the 1960s, scientists started mapping dangerous areas. Many experts worked together. They tracked places where avalanches happened. Then, they warned people to avoid those areas.

MONEY FOR RESEARCH

The first avalanche research labs started in the early 1900s. At first, they didn't get much money. However, deadly events kept happening. These events made people want to fund more research.

In some areas, signs warn people that avalanches are possible.

Avalanches often happen on slopes with angles between 30 and 45 degrees.

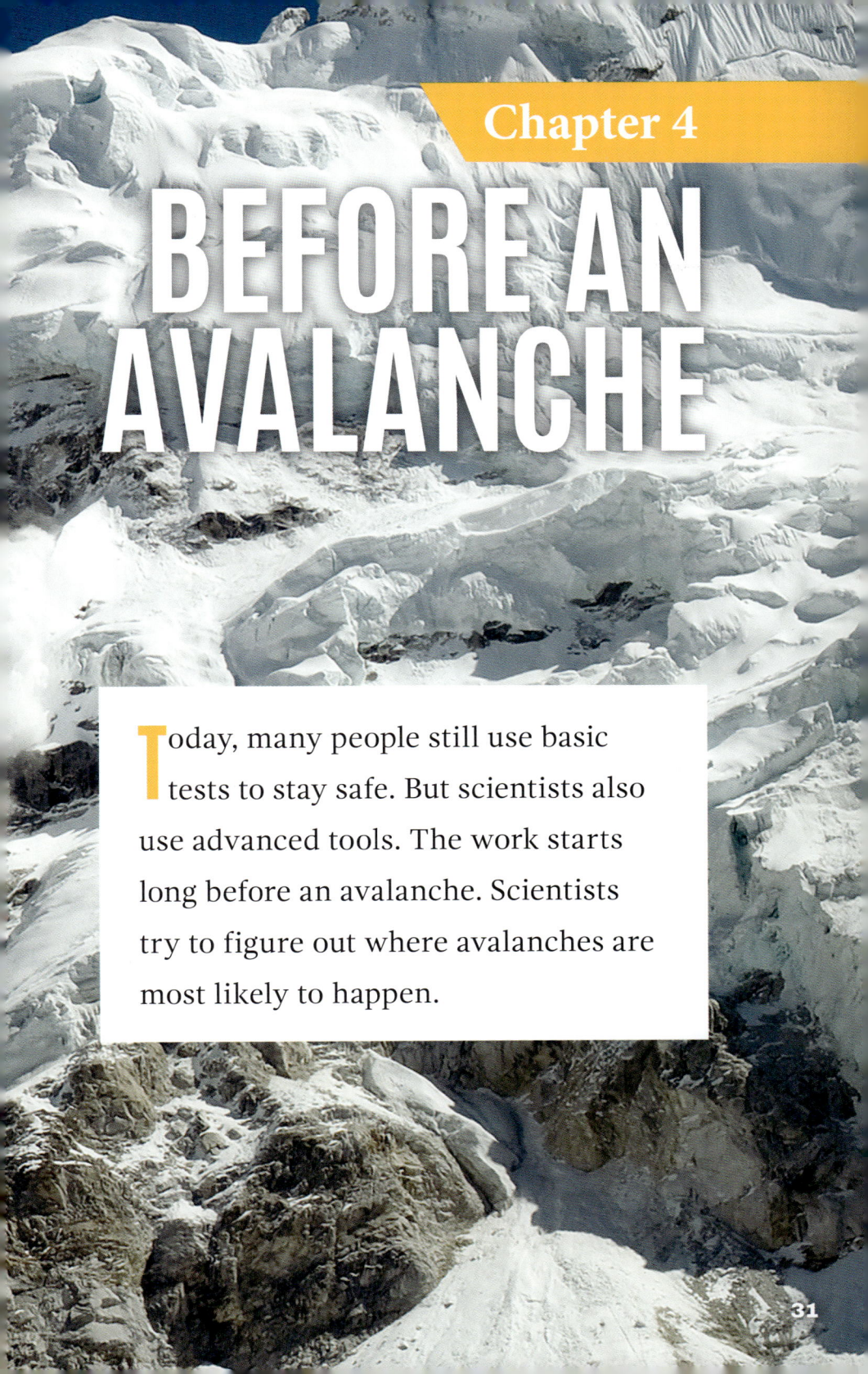

Chapter 4

BEFORE AN AVALANCHE

Today, many people still use basic tests to stay safe. But scientists also use advanced tools. The work starts long before an avalanche. Scientists try to figure out where avalanches are most likely to happen.

In the early 2000s, satellites became an important tool. They take pictures from space. That lets scientists study large areas. The satellites take pictures at different times. Then, scientists look for changes from one image to the next. For example, they look for piles of snow left by avalanches.

STRONG CAMERAS

Scientists often use satellites with strong cameras. The images show small details on a mountainside. Scientists study these details. That helps them figure out the size of an avalanche. They can also figure out its cause and its path.

There are hundreds of
satellites observing Earth.

Avalanche sensors have prevented many deaths.

Satellites help scientists find areas where many avalanches occur. Then, people put sensors in those areas. Some sensors use lasers. They take 3D measurements of a mountainside. Scientists study the measurements. They track changes in snow levels.

Other devices use radar. Radar helps scientists find out what kinds of snow and ice are on a mountainside. Some types of snow form unstable layers. These layers are more likely to become an avalanche.

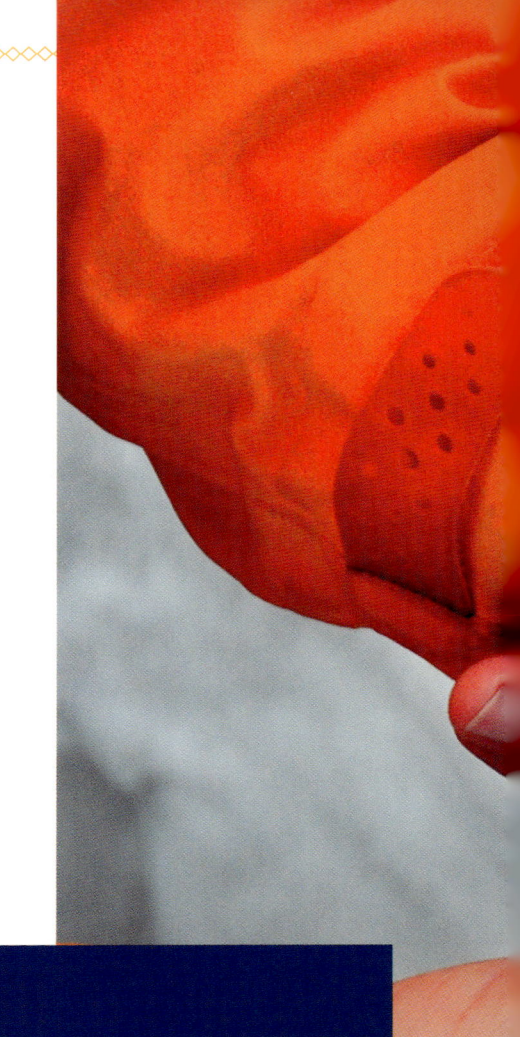

TYPES OF SNOW

Some snowflakes have six points. These flakes tend to stick together. They form stable layers. But other times, snow falls in shapes that don't stick together. This snow creates unstable layers. Unstable layers can also form when snow melts and refreezes into ice.

Crystal cards help people study the size and shape of snowflakes.

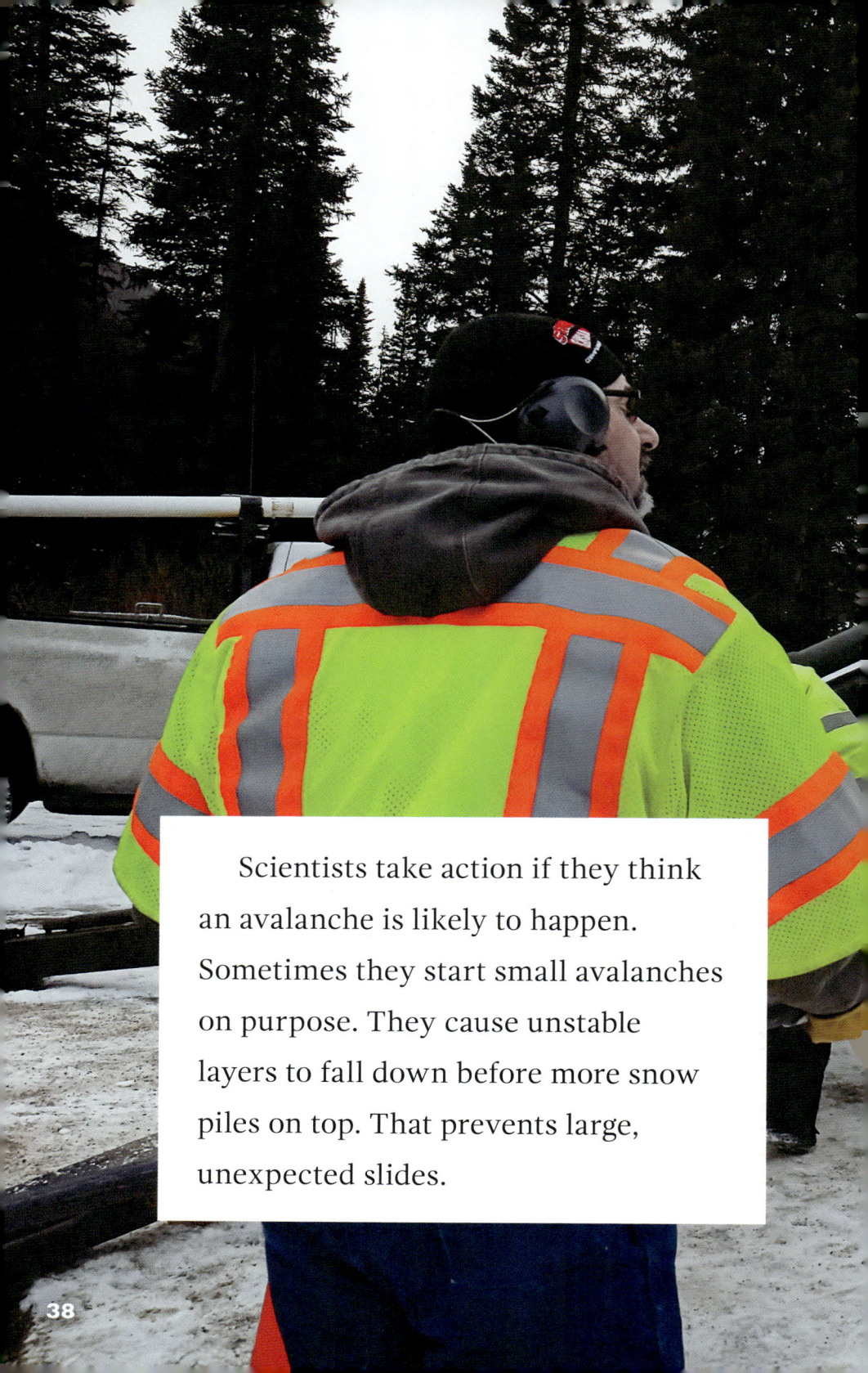

Scientists take action if they think an avalanche is likely to happen. Sometimes they start small avalanches on purpose. They cause unstable layers to fall down before more snow piles on top. That prevents large, unexpected slides.

A worker uses explosives to start a controlled avalanche in Colorado.

STARTING SLIDES

On small mountains, scientists may ski high up on a slope. From there, they can cause an avalanche on purpose. In more dangerous places, scientists may use explosives to start avalanches. They might even use large guns.

Chapter 5

DURING AN AVALANCHE

Dangerous slides can be unexpected. Slides can reach roads or towns quickly. In some places, it takes less than a minute. So, scientists must be able to detect avalanches as they happen. Then, they can warn people.

Clearing a road after an avalanche can take hours or even days.

Beacons can help rescue workers find people who are buried.

Most avalanches happen when visibility is low. Clouds and snow may block the view. Or slides may happen at night. But radar works in any weather, day or night. The sensors watch the slopes 24 hours a day. Radar can sense avalanches more than 1 mile (1.6 km) away. The sensors help scientists detect slides within a few seconds.

RADAR RESCUES

Radar is sometimes used after an avalanche, too. It can help find people trapped in snow. Radar can sense movement. Other sensors detect heat. Together, these sensors help find survivors.

Seismometers send information to machines that record the vibrations.

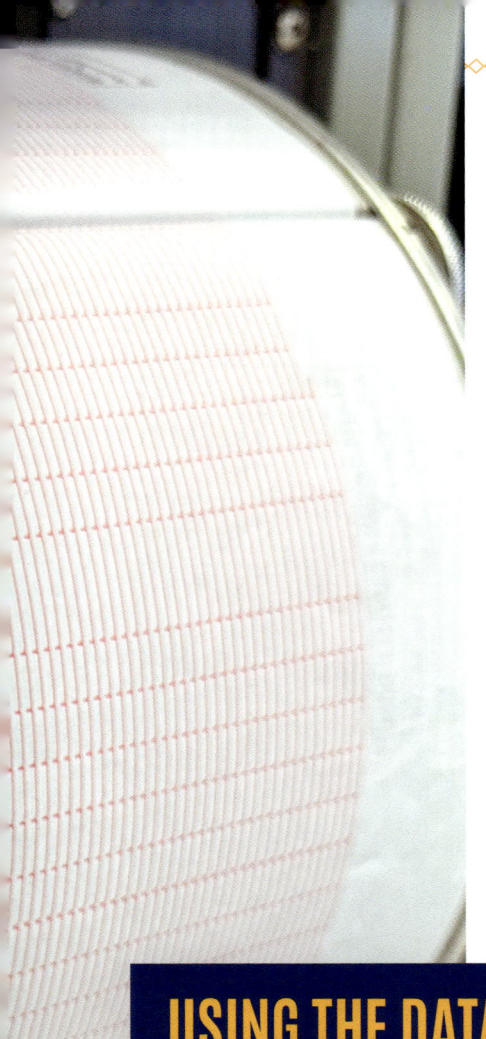

Seismometers are another important tool. Avalanches make the ground shake. Seismometers measure these vibrations. The sensors send data to computers. Then, scientists can study the data.

USING THE DATA

Seismometers give scientists helpful information. They learn the size and speed of an avalanche. The measurements also show exactly when an avalanche started. Scientists look at the weather during that time. They find out if the weather caused the slide.

Avalanches let out low sounds. Human ears cannot hear these sounds. But infrasound sensors can. Usually, scientists place infrasound sensors and seismometers around a pole. Then, they bury the pole on a mountainside.

To human ears, an avalanche sounds like rolling thunder.

WORKING TOGETHER

Infrasound sensors are good at detecting the movement of powdery snow. This is created at the start of an avalanche. Seismometers are better at sensing the movement of heavier snow at the end. Both sensors are helpful. They help detect any part of an avalanche.

BETTER WARNINGS

Some places don't have good avalanche prediction systems. This is especially true of low-income areas. It's also true of areas with few people. That can lead to dangers.

In 2015, an avalanche hit a village in Afghanistan. More than 200 people died. An engineer named Mirza Samnani wanted to help. In 2022, he helped install weather stations in several Asian countries. Each station included seven different sensors. The sensors worked together. They warned remote villages. Samnani's project saved lives.

Victims check the damage after the 2015 avalanche.

Chapter 6

NEW TECHNOLOGY

Scientists continue to get better at detecting avalanches. They are working on better sensors. And they are creating better computer models. These tools help scientists predict more avalanches. They also help send quicker warnings.

A scientist uses a water tank to test an avalanche barrier.

Drones are one new tool. These aircraft fly close to mountains. They help scientists get better measurements. Drones can use radar. They can use GPS and cameras, too. Scientists use the measurements to create better maps. Drones can also be used to start small avalanches. They can drop explosives.

FINDING PEOPLE

Drones also help find people who are trapped. Often, skiers and snowboarders wear avalanche beacons. These devices send out strong radio signals. Some drones can locate the beacons. Then rescue workers can find survivors.

Drones can go to places that are difficult for humans to reach.

Many sensors are very expensive. Scientists are working to build smaller and cheaper devices. Smaller sensors are easier to move. People can afford to build and use more of them. Using more sensors lets scientists keep track of larger areas.

SPREADING THE WORD

Scientists try to make it easier for people to find warnings. They create websites and maps. Anyone can use these resources. Scientists also lead classes. People can learn how to stay safe.

Avalanche experts teach others how to use technology to stay safe.

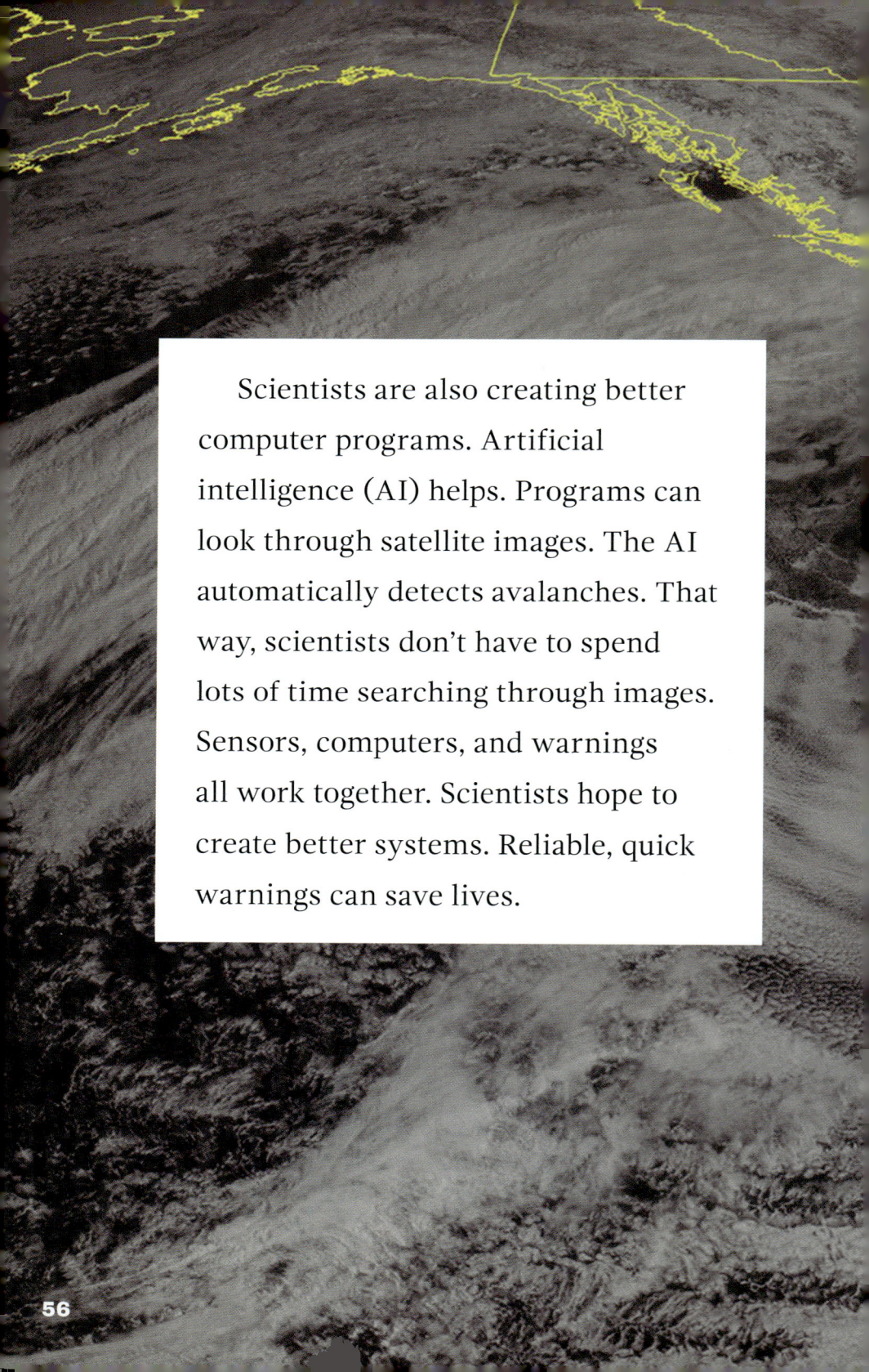

Scientists are also creating better computer programs. Artificial intelligence (AI) helps. Programs can look through satellite images. The AI automatically detects avalanches. That way, scientists don't have to spend lots of time searching through images. Sensors, computers, and warnings all work together. Scientists hope to create better systems. Reliable, quick warnings can save lives.

Satellite images helps scientists decide when to give avalanche warnings.

TIMELINE

EARLY 1900s — The first avalanche laboratories are founded.

1916 — At least 270 soldiers die in an avalanche in Italy.

1950–51 — Villages are buried, and hundreds of people die during the "Winter of Terror." It is Europe's worst avalanche season in history.

1960s — Scientists begin mapping areas where avalanches happen most often.

EARLY 2000s — Scientists begin using satellites to track avalanches.

2015 — An avalanche in Afghanistan kills more than 200 people.

2022 — Mirza Samnani helps install weather stations in remote Asian mountains.

COMPREHENSION QUESTIONS

Write your answers on a separate piece of paper.

1. Write a paragraph that explains the main ideas of Chapter 2.

2. What sensor do you think is most important for avalanche detection? Why?

3. Which devices sense the vibrations created by avalanches?

    A. inclinometers
    B. seismometers
    C. infrasound sensors

4. What would happen if scientists observed mountains with cameras but not with radar?

    A. Scientists would be able to observe mountains at any time.
    B. Scientists would be better at observing mountains in the dark.
    C. Scientists would not be able to observe mountains when it was cloudy.

5. What does **debris** mean in this book?

*It covers the road with heavy snow. Rocks and fallen trees crash down, too. The **debris** piles more than 4 feet (1.2 m) high.*

    A. unbroken objects
    B. loose pieces
    C. electronic sensors

6. What does **conditions** mean in this book?

*Avalanches only form under certain **conditions**. They need snow, a steep slope, and a trigger.*

    A. things that are not related to an event
    B. things that allow an event to happen
    C. things that are used to look at an event

Answer key on page 64.

GLOSSARY

artificial intelligence
Computer systems that can learn and change without following new instructions.

bonded
Joined or connected together.

compacts
Packs closely together.

detect
To sense or find something.

predict
To say that something will happen in the future.

programs
Lists of instructions that tell computers what to do.

radar
A system that sends out radio waves to locate objects.

retaining walls
Structures that hold back snow, soil, or other materials.

satellites
Devices that orbit Earth, often to send or collect information.

trigger
An event or action that causes something else to happen.

vibrations
Very quick back-and-forth movements.

TO LEARN MORE

BOOKS

Mitchell, K. S. *Avalanches and Landslides*. Apex Editions, 2023.

Murray, Julie. *Avalanches*. Abdo Publishing, 2025.

Petersohn, Sara. *Mountain Researchers*. Apex Editions, 2025.

ONLINE RESOURCES

Visit **www.apexeditions.com** to find links and resources related to this title.

ABOUT THE AUTHOR

Dalton Rains is an author and editor from Saint Paul, Minnesota.

INDEX

ANSWER KEY:

1. Answers will vary; 2. Answers will vary; 3. B; 4. C; 5. B; 6. B